Pebble® Plus

WHAT'S ON MyPlate?

FRUiTS on MyPlate

by Mari Schuh

Consulting Editor: Gail Saunders-Smith, PhD

Consultant: Barbara J. Rolls, PhD
Guthrie Chair in Nutrition
Pennsylvania State University
University Park, Pennsylvania

D1379120

CAPSTONE PRESS
a capstone imprint

Pebble Plus is published by Capstone Press,
1710 Roe Crest Drive, North Mankato, Minnesota 56003.
www.capstonepub.com

Copyright © 2013 by Capstone Press, a Capstone imprint. All rights reserved.
No part of this publication may be reproduced in whole or in part, or stored in a retrieval system, or transmitted
in any form or by any means, electronic, mechanical, photocopying, recording, or otherwise, without written
permission of the publisher. For information regarding permission, write to Capstone Press,
1710 Roe Crest Drive, North Mankato, MN 56003.

Library of Congress Cataloging-in-Publication Data
Quam, Mari Schuh.
 Fruit on myplate / by Mari Schuh Quam.
  p. cm.—(Pebble Plus what's on myplate?)
 Includes bibliographical references and index.
 Summary: "Simple text and photos describe USDA's MyPlate tool and healthy fruit choices for children"—Provided
by publisher.
 ISBN 978-1-4296-8741-6 (library binding)
 ISBN 978-1-4296-9412-4 (paperback)
 ISBN 978-1-62065-325-8 (eBook PDF)
 1. Fruit—Juvenile literature. I. Title. II. Title: Fruit on my plate.
 SB357.2.Q83 2013
 634—dc23   2012009308

Editorial Credits
Jeni Wittrock, editor; Sarah Bennett, designer; Svetlana Zhurkin, media researcher; Kathy McColley,
production specialist; Sarah Schuette, photo stylist; Marcy Morin, studio scheduler

Photo Credits
All photos by Capstone Studio/Karon Dubke except:
Shutterstock: brulove, cover (left), LeventeGyori, cover (right), Pinkcandy, back cover; USDA, cover (inset), 5

The author dedicates this book to Eat Right Racine's Heidi Fannin, who
is more passionate about healthy eating than anyone the author knows.

Information in this book supports
the U.S. Department of Agriculture's
MyPlate food guidance system found at
www.choosemyplate.gov. Food amounts
listed in this book are based on daily
recommendations for children ages 4-8.
The amounts listed in this book are
appropriate for children who get less than
30 minutes a day of moderate physical
activity, beyond normal daily activities.
Children who are more physically active
may be able to eat more while staying
within calorie needs. The U.S. Department
of Agriculture (USDA) does not endorse
any products, services, or organizations.

Note to Parents and Teachers

The What's on MyPlate? series supports national science standards related to health and
nutrition. This book describes and illustrates MyPlate's fruit recommendations. The images
support early readers in understanding the text. The repetition of words and phrases helps early
readers learn new words. This book also introduces early readers to subject-specific vocabulary
words, which are defined in the Glossary section. Early readers may need assistance to read
some words and to use the Table of Contents, Glossary, Read More, Internet Sites, and Index
sections of the book.

Printed in the United States of America in North Mankato, Minnesota.
112019   002925

Table of Contents

MyPlate

Fruits are a sweet part
of MyPlate.
MyPlate is a tool that
helps you eat healthy food.

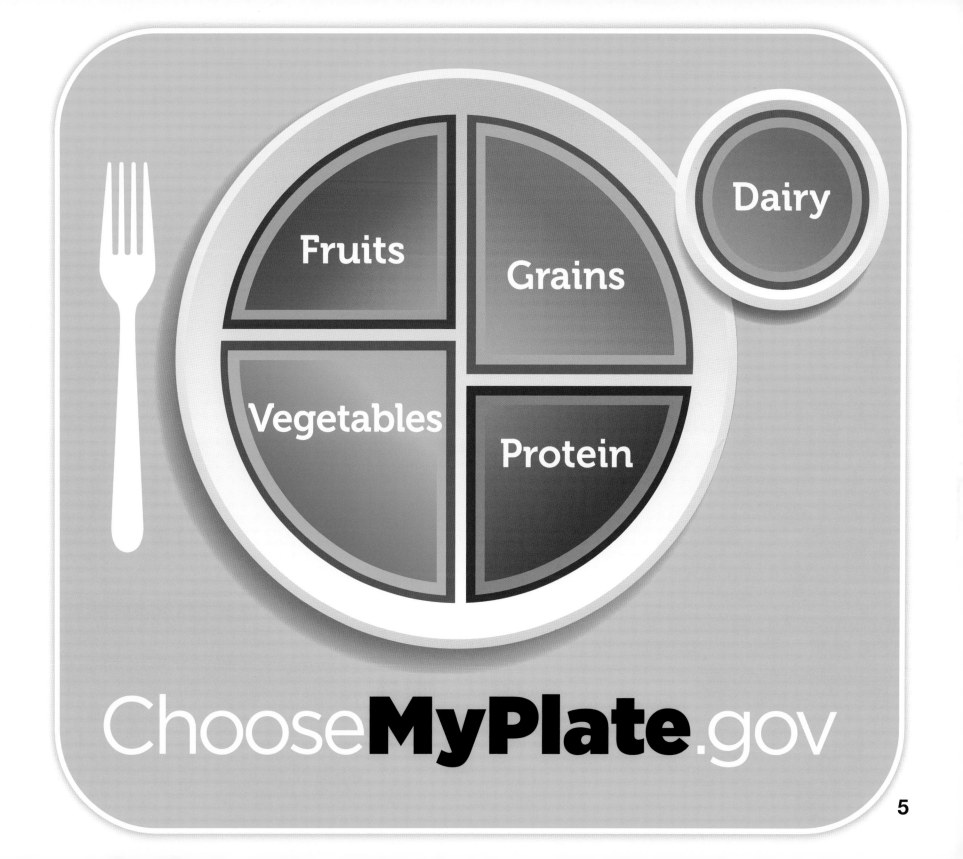

5

A healthy meal

fills half your plate

with fruits and vegetables.

Kids should eat about 1½ cups (360 milliliters) of fruit every day.

All Kinds of Fruit

Have you seen fruit growing?

Fruit grows on trees,

bushes, and vines.

Fruits have seeds.

You can eat fruit

in many ways.

Fruit can be fresh,

dried, canned, or frozen.

Eat the colors of
the rainbow. Munch on
pineapples, bananas,
grapes, and berries.

Fruit comes in

many shapes and sizes.

Try a new fruit

for lunch.

Fruit makes a great snack.

Share some fruit with a friend.

19

Healthy Eating

It's fun to try
all kinds of fruits.
What fruits will
you choose today?

How Much to Eat

Kids need to eat three servings of fruit every day. That's about 1½ cups of fruit. To get 1½ cups, pick three servings of your favorite fruits below.

½ cup (120 mL) grapes

1 small orange

½ cup (120 mL) 100-percent fruit juice

½ cup (120 mL) halved strawberries

½ cup (120 mL) pineapple chunks

¼ cup (60 mL) dried fruit

1 small banana

½ cup (120 mL) applesauce (single serving container)

Glossary

canned—sealed in a container to last longer; canned fruit that is packed in water or juice is healthier than canned fruit in syrup

dried—having most of the water taken out; people often eat dried peaches, apples, pears, plums, and figs

fruit—the fleshy, juicy part of a plant; fruit has seeds

MyPlate—a food plan that reminds people to eat healthful food and be active; MyPlate was created by the U.S. Department of Agriculture

serving—one helping of food

snack—a small amount of food people eat between meals

Read More

Aboff, Marcie. *The Fantastic Fruit Group.* MyPlate and Healthy Eating. Mankato, Minn.: Capstone Press, 2012.

Adams, Julia. *Fruits.* Good Food. New York: PowerKids Press, 2011.

Rissman, Rebecca. *Using MyPlate.* Healthy Eating with MyPlate. Chicago: Heinemann Library, 2012.

Internet Sites

FactHound offers a safe, fun way to find Internet sites related to this book. All of the sites on FactHound have been researched by our staff.

Here's all you do:

Visit *www.facthound.com*

Type in this code: 9781429687416

Super-cool stuff! Check out projects, games and lots more at www.capstonekids.com

Index

Word Count: 121
Grade: 1
Early-Intervention Level: 14